WEE FOLKS STORIES

FROM

THE NEW TESTAMENT

WEE FOLKS STORIES

FROM

THE NEW TESTAMENT

MOSTLY IN WORDS OF ONE SYLLABLE

ELIZABETH ROBINSON SCOVIL

Updated by Jonathan Savage, Esq.
Edited by Mikesch Muecke, Ph.D.

Biblical Note:
The words of Jesus Christ printed in this book are depicted
as in the Holy Bible – New International Version – and are
highlighted in red.

Hog Press
an imprint of Culicidae Press
PO Box 5069
Madison, WI 53705-5069
USA
hogpress.com
editor@hogpress.com
+1 (352) 388-3848
+1 (515) 462-0278

WEE FOLKS STORIES FROM THE NEW TESTAMENT: MOSTLY IN WORDS OF ONE SYLLABLE
2024 © Elizabeth Robinson Scovil
Edited by Jon Savage and Mikesch Muecke

All rights reserved. No part of this work covered by the copyright hereon may be reproduced or used in any form or by any means—graphic, electronic, or mechanical, including photocopying, recording, taping, or information storage and retrieval systems—without written permission of the publisher. Neither the author nor the publisher make any representation, express or implied, with regard to the accuracy of the information contained in this book and cannot accept any legal responsibility or liability for any errors or omissions that may be made.

ISBN: 978-1-941892-82-4

Our books may be purchased in bulk for promotional, educational or business use. Please contact your local bookseller or the Hog Press Sales Department at +1-515-462-0278 or email us at sales@hogpress.com

x.com/culicidaepress – facebook.com/culicidaepress

Book layout and design by polytekton ©2024, based on the original by Elizabeth Robinson Scovil
Background photo on cover by Félix Bonfils (1831-1885), *General View of Jerusalem* [*Vue générale de Jérusalem*]

Table of Contents

Preface	6
Christ Is Born	9
The Wise Men	13
Christ In The Temple	15
Christ When A Man	19
Christ Blesses The Children	22
Christ Feeds The Hungry	25
Christ Cures The Sick	27
Christ Gives Sight To The Blind	31
The Deaf And Mute Man	33
The Lame Man	35
The Girl Who Was Dead	39
The Prodigal Son	41
Christ On The Cross	45
Christ Rose From The Dead	49
Proof Of The Holy Spirit	53
The Kind Woman	57
Coloring Pages	60

Preface

The original of this text was written by Ms. Elizabeth Robinson Scovil, and was published and copyrighted in 1921.

The book was re-printed in the early 1930s.

Ms. Scovil's intent was to write a book of mostly one syllable words so that the youngest of children (the 'wee folks') could better hear, read and understand the messages from some favorite and critical New Testament stories.

The text and pictures of this book mirror Ms. Scovil's original publication, with only a few changes to reflect our contemporary language. Truly, this is her book more than a century after her original publication.

Ms. Scovil (1849 – 1934) was a truly remarkable woman for the ages. To learn more about Ms. Elizabeth Robinson Scovil, go to http://bit.ly/scovil

The original title of this book was *Wee Folks Stories From The New Testament – In Words of One Syllable,* a title we kept while adding the word 'Mostly' because there are some required two-syllable words in the text as well.

Jonathan dedicates the efforts related to this book to his grandchildren, and the children and grandchildren of Jonathan's sister Judy, his brother Rick, and his adoptive sister Joy. Joy is now in heaven.

Mikesch dedicates the efforts related to this book to his family, his partner, and her children and grandchildren.

Christ Is Born

We are all glad when Christmas comes. It is the birthday of our Lord Jesus Christ. We give gifts to those we love, for on that day God gave us His son to live in this world and teach all of us how to live here and how to die. His mother Mary's home was in a small place called Nazareth. She went with Joseph, her husband, to pay a tax, to Bethlehem, which was once King David's town.

There was such a crowd there that the inn was full, and they could find no place to stay. So, they went to a large cave where the cattle were kept. Here was a stone trough in which the food for the beasts was put, and there, when her child was born, Mary laid Him, well wrapped up from the cold.

Just outside the town there were some men who kept a flock of sheep. On this night, while they watched the flock, a bright light shone around them, and a great fear fell on them. Then they heard the voice of an angel, which said to them, "Do not be afraid, I bring you good news of a great joy, that will be for all people. Today in the town of David a Savior has been born to you; He is Christ the Lord. This will be a sign to you: you will find a Baby wrapped in cloths and lying in a manger." At once there was with the angel a host of angels, who sang, "Glory to God in the highest, and on earth peace on earth to whom His favor rests."

The men who kept the sheep said, "Let us go to Bethlehem and see this thing that has happened, which the Lord has told us about."

They went with haste and found Mary and Joseph and the Babe, as they had been told they should. They went out and spread the news that Christ had come to earth. All who heard these strange things were filled with awe. Mary thought of these things in her heart, but did not talk about them. The men who took care of the sheep praised God for all they had heard and seen.

The Wise Men

The Jewish people had known for a long time that God would send a prince to be their king. At the time Christ was born, they thought this king would come soon, and Wise Men from the East had come to Jerusalem to look for him. A bright star went in front of them and led them on. At last, it stood still and shone down on the place where Jesus lay in the arms of His mother.

He was the Son of God, but He chose to be born in this world as a child so that He might grow up to be a man and teach us how both young and old ought to live and love in this life.

The three Wise Men went in and knelt before the young child and showed the gifts they had brought for Him, gold and myrrh and a gum that gives out a strong, sweet smell when it is burned. Their joy was great that they had found Him.

Herod, the king who ruled the Jewish people, was full of rage when he heard that the Wise Men had seen the Christ, for whom they had looked so long. He meant to kill Him. So, he said that no child less than two years old should live in the whole land; they should all be killed.

God sent His angel to tell Joseph in a dream that Herod meant to kill the young Child and Joseph must save Him. So, he took Mary and the Babe and left by night for Egypt to hide Him from Herod. They stayed there till Herod himself was dead.

Christ In The Temple

The temple was to the Jewish people what a church is to us. The first time that Mary took her Child there was when He was one month and ten days old. God had told the Jewish people that when a child was born it should be brought to His house and bring a gift with it. The rich brought a lamb, and the poor a dove. Mary was not rich, so she took a pair of doves.

There was an old man in the temple whose name was Simeon. He was a good man and God told him that he should not die till he had seen Christ. When Mary brought in the young Christ child, he took Him in his arms and blessed Him, and said that it was He who should save Israel.

Then Anna, a woman prophet, who came to the temple by night, as well as by day, to pray, when she saw the Christ child, she gave thanks to God that she had seen the Christ, and told all those who had hoped He was near, that He had come.

When Herod was dead, Mary and Joseph brought our Lord back from Egypt, and they lived in Nazareth.

When Christ Jesus was twelve years old, they went with Him to Jerusalem, to the temple, to a great feast that the Jewish people held each year. When it was time for them to go home, they set out with their friends. At the end of the first day, when they camped for the night, Christ was not to be found. They had thought all day that He was with some of their friends. When they knew He was not with their friends, they turned back to Jerusalem, and after a three-day search, they found Him in the temple.

There were wise men there who talked to Him and He to them. They could not think how such a young boy could know so much of the Law and the deep things of God. They did not know that He was the Son of God, sent into the world to teach the truth to all who would learn it.

When Joseph and Mary found Him, Mary said "Son, why have you treated us so? Behold, your father and I have been searching for you in great distress." He said to her, "Why were you searching for me? Didn't you know that I had to be in my Father's house?" He then went home to Nazareth and worked for years with Joseph at his trade.

Christ When A Man

Jesus grew tall and strong year by year till He was a man. He was more wise than other men and all who knew Him loved Him. When He was thirty years old, He began to preach, and told those who heard Him to give up their sins and love God and try to please Him.

One day as He walked by the Sea of Galilee and He saw Simon Peter and Andrew his brother, as they cast a net in the sea to catch fish. He told them to come with Him and that they should help save the souls of all people. They left their nets at once and went with Him. He called two more brothers, James and John, who were in a boat at work at their nets. In the end Christ had twelve disciples, men who were with Him all the time, but these were the first four.

Once when He taught them He said, "Blessed are the pure in heart, for they will see God." He told them to give to those in need and to do good to those who were not kind to them and win them over with love.

Jesus said that those who heard Him and did what He said, were like a wise man who dug deep and built his house on a rock. When the rain fell and the floods came and the wind blew, it stood firm. They who heard and would not do right were like a man who built his house on the sand; the rain came and the waves beat on that house and it fell down with a great crash.

Christ Blesses The Children

Jesus liked to help all who were poor, or sick, or sad. He healed those who had faith in Him and who knew that He would cure them.

One day the friends of some young children brought them to Him that he might bless them. The disciples were shocked; they thought all His time should be spent in grave talk with those who were grown up. But Christ loved the little ones, and He was not happy that the disciples tried to keep them from Him. He said, "Let the little children come to Me, do not hinder them, for the kingdom of heaven belongs to such as these." Then He took them up in His arms, put His hands on them, and blessed them.

How glad their mothers must have been to know that Jesus loved the babies and, though He was the Son of God, He was not too great, nor so full of care for what He had to do for the rest of the world, that He could not take time to bless them too. He loves each child just as much still, though we can not see Him now.

All their lives those children must have thought of that kind face, with its look of love. It must have helped them to do right when they might have done wrong and made them more fit to live with Him in His home in heaven when they died.

Jesus said once that none but those who were pure in heart, like a good child, could hope to see God when they left this world. He can not bring to heaven those who like to keep bad thoughts on their minds.

Christ Feeds The Hungry

Jesus loved to teach all who would come to hear Him. Sometimes, great crowds came, more than could squeeze into a large church, so they sat on the side of a hill, or on the shore of the lake, while Jesus talked with them.

Once they stayed for such a long time that they grew weak for want of food. The disciples begged Jesus to send the crowd home, as they could not get food where they were. Jesus said "You give them something to eat?" They said, "We have no more than five barley loaves and two small fish, but what are they for these crowds."

Jesus said, "Have them sit down." There was much grass in the place, so the people sat down. Some five thousand of them. Jesus took the loaves and when He had thanked God, He gave them to those who were set down and the fish too, as much as they could eat.

When they were done Jesus told His disciples to pick up all that was left, so there would be no waste. They filled twelve baskets; there was much more left than there had been at first.

Then the men when they had seen what Jesus had done, said, "Surely this is the prophet who is come into the world."

It may be that the five barley loaves and the two small fish were the lunch that a boy brought from home when he came to hear Jesus speak. If so, what pride he must have felt all his life that Jesus had used them to work this great miracle.

Christ Cures The Sick

    Where Christ lived, a house is built with a flat roof and a kind of thatch on it that is not hard to tear up. One day, as Jesus talked in the upstairs room of a house, four men brought a sick man in a bed in hopes our Lord would make him well. The throng was so great that they could not get him in the house, so they took his bed up a stairs and laid him on the roof. They tore out part of the roof and let him down at Jesus' feet.

    Jesus knew that they must have much faith to be so sure that He could cure their friend. He said to the sick man, "Friend, your sins are forgiven." Some of the scribes who had come to hear Him said to themselves, "Who can forgive sins but God alone." They said that

Jesus was a bad man to try to make them think He was God.

Jesus knew their thoughts and said "Why are you thinking these things in your hearts? Which is easier to say 'Your sins are forgiven' or to say 'Get up and walk'". Then He said to the sick man, "I tell you get up, take your mat and go home." The man at once got on his feet, rolled up the mats on which he had lain, and walked home.

All who saw this great deed praised God and knew that He was the Christ or it could not have been done. They did not yet know that He was the Son of God.

Christ Gives Sight To The Blind

More than once Jesus gave back sight to those who were blind.

One day He saw a man who had been blind from his birth. He went up to the man and spoke to him. Then He wet a small piece of clay and made it soft and laid it on the blind man's eyes. He said to him, "Go, wash in the Pool of Siloam." The blind man went and washed. When he came out of the pool, he could see.

Those who knew him when he was blind said, "Isn't this the same man who used to sit and beg?." Some claimed that he was. Some said, "No. He only looks like him." The man said, "I am he." So, they asked him how he was cured. He said, "A man that is called Jesus made clay and put it on my eyes and said to me, 'Go to the pool of Siloam and wash.' I went and washed and got my sight." They said, "Where is He?" The man said "I am the man."

There were people who were full of hate of Jesus and said they did not think the man had been blind. So, they went to his parents and said to them, "Is this your son … is this the one you say was born blind? How is it that now he can see?" They feared the crowd, so they said, "He is of age; he will speak for himself."

The man told them all the facts once more, and said, "Nobody has ever heard of opening the eyes of a man born blind. If this man were not from God, He could do nothing." But the crowd would not hear him.

The Deaf And Mute Man

One day Jesus walked by the Sea of Galilee, and a poor man was brought to Him who was deaf and mute.

He would not hear his friends speak, nor the birds sing, nor all the sweet sounds that fill the air on a fine day. When the storm raged and the wind blew down great trees, he could see them fall and could not hear them crash. All was quiet for him. He did not know the sound of a laugh, nor the soft notes of a song, nor the kind voice that tried to bring him ease when he was sad.

He could make his wants known by signs; a shake of the head when he meant no, and a nod when he would say yes. But he could not speak words of love to those whom he loved best, nor hear them when they spoke to him. How sad his life must have been!

His friends heard of Jesus, who had made the blind see and the lame to walk. They thought He could help their poor friend; so they brought him to our Lord and begged Him to put His hands on him.

Jesus took him to one side out of the crowd and put His fingers in his ears and touched his tongue and looked up to God and said "Be opened." At once the man heard and spoke. How full of joy he must have been and how glad his friends were that they had brought him to Jesus.

They said, "He has done all things well; He makes both the deaf to hear and the mute to speak."

The Lame Man

At the time of one of the feasts of the Jewish people, Jesus went to Jerusalem. There, near a place where sheep were sold, was a pool called Bethesda, with five gates, each with its own porch, that led down to it. In there lay sick and lame and blind folk. At a fixed time each day an angel came and stirred the pool; the one who first stepped in when it had been stirred was cured.

Jesus saw a man who had been there for a long time while he waited to be made well. He said to him, "Do you want to get well?" The man said, "Sir, I have no one to help me into the pool when the water is stirred. While I am trying to get in, someone else goes down ahead of me." Jesus said to him, "Get up. Pick up your mat and walk." The man got up and walked; he was cured. Jesus said to him, "See, you are well again. Stop sinning or something worse may happen to you."

When some men came to ask Jesus if it was true that He was the Son of God, He told them to look at the works that He had done. He gave the blind sight, healed the sick, made the deaf hear and the lame walk, and raised the dead to life. No one but God could have done these things just by a few words. While He was on earth, He tried to help the sick and sad and to make men cease from sin and do what was right in the sight of God.

The Girl Who Was Dead

One of the Jewish people, named Jairus, had a child who was ill. He knew that Jesus had cured the sick, so he went to Him, for he feared his child would die and no one could save her.

When he saw our Lord, he fell at His feet and begged Him to come with him to his house. He said, "My little girl lies at the point of death; I pray thee come and lay Thy hands on her that she may be healed, and live."

Jesus went with him and a great crowd went too. While He was on the way, someone came to Jairus' house and said, "Your daughter is dead. Don't bother the Teacher any more."

As soon as Jesus heard this, He turned to Jairus and said, "Don't be afraid; just believe, and she will be healed." When He came to the house all were in great grief. When He went in, He said to those who wept, "Stop wailing. She is not dead, but asleep." They laughed and said "She is dead."

Then Jesus sent them all out of the house but Jairus and his wife and three of His own disciples, Peter, James and John, whom He had brought with Him, and went to the sick girl's room. He took her by the hand and said, "My child, get up!" She got up and walked, and Jesus told them to give her something to eat.

The Prodigal Son

We all like to hear a story. Jesus used to teach His disciples in this way, by means of what are called parables.

One that He told them was of the two sons who lived at home. One day the youngest son said, "Father, give me my share of the estate." So, he took his share and went to a far land and spent all that he had just as he pleased.

When all he had was spent, he found himself so poor that he had no food to eat. He went to work for a man who sent him into the fields to feed the swine. He was so starved that he was glad to eat from the husks that were fed to the pigs, as no one would give him food.

Then he began to think of all the good things he had at home. He said to himself, "How many of my father's hired men have food to spare, and here I am starving to death. I will set out and go back to my father and say to him; Father, I have sinned against heaven and you. I am no longer worthy to be called your son; make me like one of your hired men."

So he went, but when he was yet a great way off his father saw him and ran to meet him and put his arms around his neck and kissed him. The son said, "Father, I have sinned against heaven and you. I am no longer worthy to be called your son."

But the father said to those in the house, "Quick! Bring the best robe and put it on him. Put a ring on his finger and sandals on his feet. Bring the fattened calf and kill it. Let's have a feast and celebrate. For this son of mine was dead and is alive again; he was lost and is found. So they began to celebrate."

Now the elder son was in the field at work; when he came in and heard the songs and saw the dance. He asked what it all meant. One of the men told him that his father had the fat calf killed, he was so pleased his young son had got home safe and sound. The brother was mad and would not go in.

His father came out and begged him to come in to the feast. He said, "Look! All these years I've been slaving for you and never disobeyed your orders. Yet you never gave me even a young goat so I could celebrate with my friends. But when this son of yours who has squandered your property with prostitutes comes home, you kill the fattened calf for him."

The father said, "My son. You are always with me and everything I have is yours. But we had to celebrate and be glad, because this brother of yours was dead and is alive again; he was lost and is found."

Christ On The Cross

Some of the Jewish people were full of hate of Jesus and they made up their minds to kill Him. They told the Romans, who ruled their land at this time, that Christ wished to be king of the Jews and drive the Romans out. This was not true, but the chief priests and the scribes made Pilate, the Roman ruler, think that it was.

They asked Judas, one of our Lord's own disciples, to show the men, who were sent to take Him, where he was. Judas said he would do so.

Our Lord loved to talk to God. He knew now that the hour was near when He would be put to death. So, He went to the Mount of Olives, and where the great trees stood close side by side, and He knelt down to

pray. We may be sure that God heard Him and gave Him strength for all He had to go through.

At last a crowd of men, led by Judas, came to take Him. Judas drew near to kiss Him, for this was the sign he had told the men he would give them. Jesus said, "Judas, are you betraying the Son of Man with a kiss?"

Then they led Him to Pilate. The people told Pilate that by their laws Jesus ought to die, for He said that He was the Son of God. Pilate said, "I find no basis for a charge against this man… I have found in Him no basis for the death penalty." But the people with loud cries begged that He should be nailed to the cross.

So, He who had been so kind to all and had done so much good and was God's Son, whom God had sent in the world, was put to a death of shame, as if He had been a thief, or had killed a man.

When Christ died it was dark for three hours in all the land. Those who stood near the cross where He hung, knew that He was the Son of God.

His friends took His body and wrapped it in a linen cloth with spice, and laid it in a new tomb, carved out of a rock, and rolled a great rock to the door of the tomb and left Him. They did not know that their woe was to be turned to joy.

Christ Rose From The Dead

On the first day of the week, before the sun was up, so it was yet dark, one of Jesus' friends, named Mary Magdelene, went to the tomb where He had been laid.

As she drew near, she saw that the rock which had closed the tomb had been rolled to one side. Then she ran to where Peter and John were and said, "We were asked by an angel 'Why do you look for the living among the dead? He is not here. He has risen!'"

Peter and John went back to the grave with her. John stooped down and looked in. He saw the linen cloth in which our Lord had been wrapped and the shroud that had been round his head, but He was not there. They went home, but Mary stayed and still wept and looked more in the tomb.

There she saw two angels, one at the head and one at the foot of the place where Jesus had lain. They

asked her why she cried. She told them she did not know where the Lord had gone.

When she had said this, she turned and saw Jesus at her side. She did not know Him. She thought He was the gardener. He said to her, "Mary." Then she knew Him and cried. "Master." He said, "Do not hold on to me, for I have not yet returned to the Father. Go instead to my brothers and tell them 'I am returning to my Father and your Father, to my God and your God.'" So, Mary went and told them.

Our Lord stayed on earth for forty more days and showed Himself often to the disciples. It was hard to make one of them, Thomas, think it was our Lord Himself, for Thomas had seen Him die. At last, when he had felt the print of the nails on our Lord's hands, where He had been nailed on the cross, he said that it was in truth his own Master who rose from the dead.

In His last days on earth Jesus taught His disciples much that they were to do when He had left them. At the end of forty days, as they all stood with Him, He rose in the air and a cloud hid Him from their sight. He had gone to live with God, where we hope to go too when we die.

Proof Of The Holy Spirit

When our Lord had left this world and gone to live with God, the men who had been with Him for so long were sad: they missed His love and care for them. He had once said that, when He had to go, God would send a Comforter to guide and help them. This is the Holy Spirit that lives in our hearts to help us do right and to feel sad when we do wrong. We all know what is right, though there are times when we do not want to do it. If we ask God to help us not sin, He will help us to flee from bad thoughts, or not to speak the mean words that rise on out lips.

One day these friends of Christ were all in one place. They may have come there to talk of Christ, and tell Him they missed Him, and to pray to Him to send them a sign that He was still near them.

As they sat still there came a sound as of a great wind that rushed past them and filled all the house. Then they saw something bright like a flame or tongue of fire, that sat on the head of each one. The Bible says they were filled with the Holy Spirit, and each of them could speak new languages they had not known until then.

At this time there were in Jerusalem a large band of people who had come from far lands to have a great feast which Jewish people held each year. It was called the Feast of Weeks and was kept while some of the grain was reaped and stored. These people did not all speak the same kind of words and so did not know what was meant when they tried to talk to each other.

But those on whom the tongues of fire had been on their heads could talk to these men in words they knew, and could tell them the great news that the Son of God had gone out of sight but He was still glad to help all who would ask Him to do so.

The people were full of awe and said, "Are not all these that speak Galileans? How hear we words in our own tongue wherein we were born?" They did not know that God had done this strange thing so they could be told of our Lord's life and death.

The Kind Woman

Joppa was a town on the sea, forty miles from Jerusalem. Men who sailed in ships went back and forth in its streets and there was much life there. Goods from all parts of the then known world were brought to it. Once when the Jewish people built a great temple to God, the strange rare woods for it were floated by sea to Joppa and sent from there to Jerusalem.

It was not a small or mean town. Yet, we know the names of only a few of those who filled the streets and went here and there on their tasks day by day. One name that has come down to us through all the years have passed since it was a large sea port, is that of a woman.

She was called Tabitha by the Jewish people and Dorcas by the Greek people who lived in the town and knew her. The name meant the same in the language which each spoke, though it does not sound the same. It means a kind of deer that has large bright eyes. Dorcas' eyes may have been large and soft; I am sure that they were kind and true.

We are not told that Dorcas was rich, or pretty to see, but that she did good deeds to those who were near her, and gave them all she could spare. One day Dorcas was sick; she may have been tired out by all she had done and did not have enough strength to get well, and she died.

Her friends heard that Christ's disciple Peter was at a place called Lydda, not far from Joppa, and he had cured the sick there. So, although they knew she was dead, they sent for him. When he came they took him to the room where Dorcas lay. Some of those for whom she had worked stood around Peter. They felt they had lost a best friend: they cried and showed Peter the coats and other things she had made for them.

Peter said they must go out of the room, for the room must be still and quiet. When they were gone, he knelt down and prayed; then he turned to Dorcas, took her hand, and said, "Dorcas, rise." She opened her eyes, and when she saw Peter, she sat up. Then Peter called her friends and gave her back to them, to their great joy and happiness.

The End

Your child (or you) can color in the images from the book on the next pages. Enjoy!

www.ingramcontent.com/pod-product-compliance
Lightning Source LLC
Chambersburg PA
CBHW052123070526
44586CB00016B/2057